Insight Text Guide

Brigid Magner

Blueprints for a Barbed-Wire Canoe

Wayne Macauley

Insight Publications

First published in 2005, reprinted 2006.

Insight Publications Pty Ltd
ABN 57 005 102 983
128 Balcombe Road
Mentone
Victoria 3194
Australia.
Tel: 61 3 9583 5839
Fax: 61 3 9583 9573
Email: books@insightpublications.com.au

www.insightpublications.com.au

Cover Design: Graphic Partners
Internal Design: Sarn Potter
DTP: Set in 9.5/14pt Optima by SPG
Series Editor: Robert Beardwood
Editing: Carole Pearce
Printed by Hyde Park Press, South Australia

National Library of Australia Cataloguing-in-Publication data:
Magner, Brigid, 1971–
Wayne Macauley's Blueprint for a barbed-wire canoe.
ISBN 1 920693 98 X.
1. Macauley, Wayne. Blueprints for a barbed-wire canoe. 2.
Macauley, Wayne. – Criticism and interpretation. (Series : Insight text guide).

A823.3

CHARACTER MAP

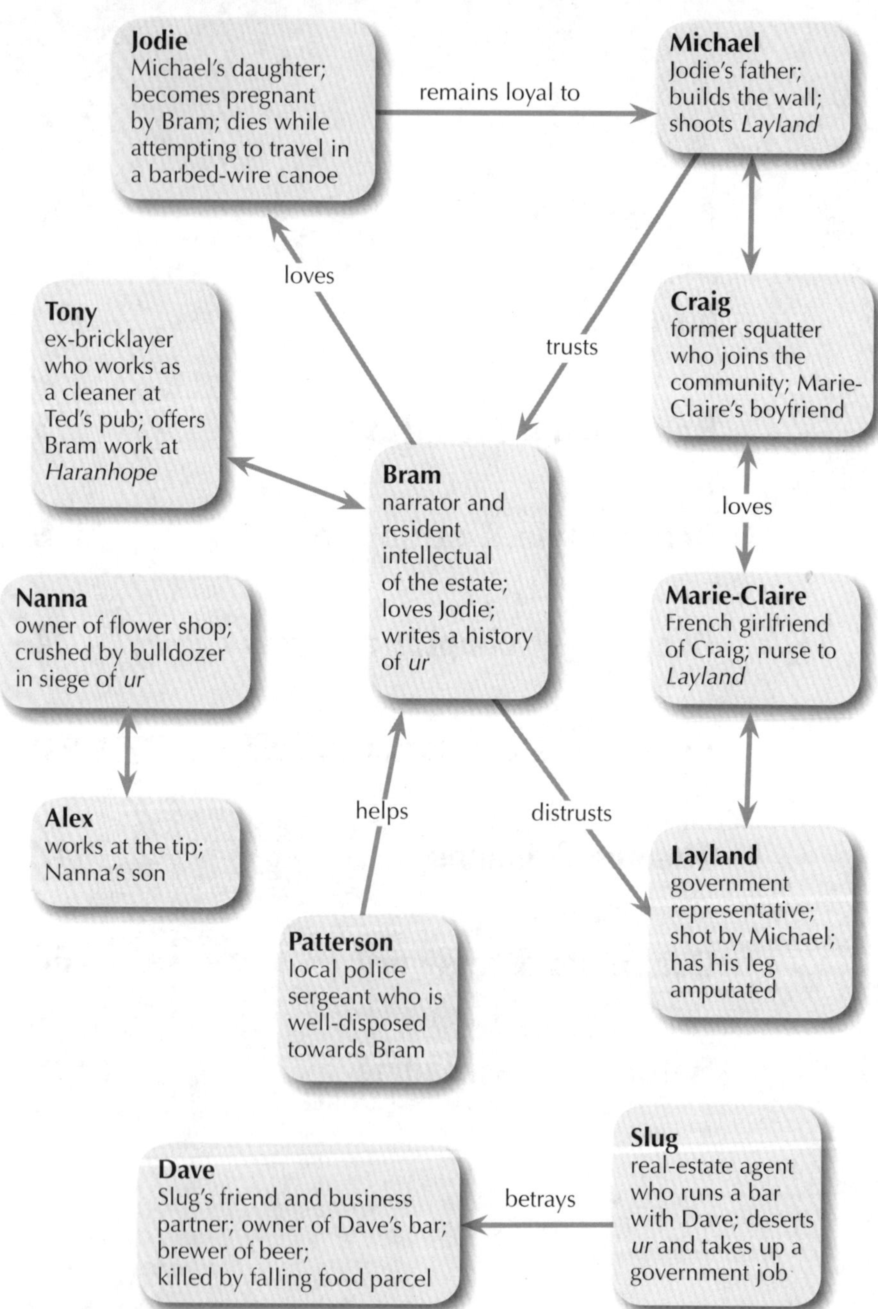

contents

INTRODUCTION

Blueprints for a Barbed-Wire Canoe, published in 2004, is a novel about '*ur*', a failed housing experiment on the outer edges of Melbourne. It tells the story of an estate that is victimised by the neglect of the local authorities, besieged by vandals and threatened by a freeway development. Those residents who do not leave in the initial period of decline become part of a close-knit community, within which the bonds between people are repeatedly put to the test, revealing their concern for each other, The various deprivations the residents endure reduce them to feral scavengers rather than the urban sophisticates they intended to be when they moved into the estate. Bram, the narrator, is the only one left at the end. Seeking to make sense of his experience, Bram writes the history of the estate, filling in the gaps with his own fictions.

The blueprints of the novel's title refer to a set of designs for a canoe made of barbed wire that are handed down to Bram's girlfriend, Jodie, by her father. These blueprints symbolise a certain fatalism and independence in the face of life's absurdities. Perhaps in response to the failure of the estate and her father's increasing madness, Jodie puts the plans into action, bringing the history of *ur* to a tragic close. Through her watery death, Jodie becomes the ultimate victim of a housing project gone wrong.

Blueprints for a Barbed-Wire Canoe may be read as an elegy for the suburban dream, which is revealed to be a mere illusion. The novel questions the Australian desire to build houses on all available land, by showing how this endless expansion can impact on the lives of hapless individuals. The author depicts a community created through shared hardship that is eventually destroyed by the authorities that originally built the estate. While the residents may be powerless to stop this happening, they show considerable inventiveness in their attempts to survive increasing depredation. Long after it is reasonable to do so, the inhabitants of the estate continue to superimpose their hopes onto this

dystopian landscape. Jodie's final gesture marks the end of this optimism in a spectacular fashion. This event signals a change of direction for Bram, essentially bringing the entire narrative to an end.

Wayne Macauley's novel contributes to an ongoing concern with the nature of suburban life in the Australian literary tradition, and in Australian society at large. It may be read as a metaphor for white settlement in Australia and the efforts of Europeans to impose their culture on a wild, inhospitable land. As Guy Rundle observes, the novel reflects 'an absolute fear that running beneath the way we live ... there is nothing but sand and desert'.[1]

1 Rundle, Guy launch speech, http://members.dodo.com.au/~ghannah/macauleybfabwc.html.

BACKGROUND & CONTEXT

About the author

Wayne Macauley is a Melbourne writer whose stories have been published in *Meanjin, Westerly, Overland, Arena, HQ* and other magazines. He was the winner of *The Age* Short Story Competition in 1995 and was anthologised in *Best Australian Stories 2001*. He has written extensively for the theatre over many years and was a founding member of the award-winning site-specific performance company, the *Institute of Complex Entertainment*. He has recently held an Australia Council grant to complete a collection of short fiction. His second novel, *Caravan Story*, was published in 2005.

Macauley was inspired to write *Blueprints for a Barbed-Wire Canoe* as a result of his experiences living on the fringes of Melbourne. While the book was written ten years ago,[2] its subject matter is perhaps even more relevant in the early years of the twenty-first century, given the ongoing urban sprawl across available land. He has described the plot of the novel as being concerned with 'issues of urban planning and Australia's need to take up all the empty space that's available'. The novel, he claims, tackles the idea that 'everyone should own a house, no matter what the cost'.[3]

Raised in an outer-suburban landscape which has inspired much of his creative output, Macauley describes the place in which he was brought up as 'the edge of the known universe': a place 'where the new houses and big furniture showrooms fall over into dead paddocks and scrub'. He has said that 'the landscape of your first independent experiences – the first time you really start thinking for yourself – becomes the imaginative landscape into which you then, as a writer, go rambling'. He expresses ambivalence about the place he comes from, yet he believes that he must make the most of this material because it's what he knows best: 'in the end

2 Kyriacou, Kate 'Writer tells of urban myth', Moreland Leader, 15 March 2004, http://members.dodo.com.au/~ghannah/macauleybfabwc.html#Interview.

3 Kyriacou, Kate http://members.dodo.com.au/~ghannah/macauleybfabwc.html#Interview.

you've got to work with what you're given', he observes.[4] Acknowledging that his imaginative landscape was closer to home and less prepossessing than the Left Bank of Paris enabled Macauley to eventually find his own creative voice.

4 Macauley Wayne, 'Where do I come from?', speech given at the Melbourne International Writers Festival 2004, 22 August 2004, http://members.dodo.com.au/~ghannah/macauley.html.

Precursors to *Blueprints for a Barbed-Wire Canoe*

A great deal has been written about the urbanised nature of Australia. In Australian literature, the desert/bush landscape often figures as an idealised Australia, whereas the city is frequently seen as less authentic. The characters who live in *ur* must deal with the wildness in their community and the decay and degradation their isolation has produced. Neither urbanites nor bush dwellers, the residents of *ur* inhabit an in-between space which has not been thoroughly explored in Australian literature.

According to Guy Rundle, *Blueprints for a Barbed-Wire Canoe* has much in common with the work of D. H. Lawrence, David Ireland and Peter Carey.[5] These writers have produced works which explore themes of 'nothingness' in Australia. Early British immigrants who could not relate to the local landscape saw it as a 'terra nullius', or an empty land waiting to be filled. For the original inhabitants of the land, however, the country is full of meaning – a quality which was invisible to the first European settlers.

While Aboriginal people are absent from this story, their shadow falls across it in significant ways. The residents of *ur* might be understood as being symbolic of the folly of white habitation in Australia. They fail to understand their surroundings, fruitlessly trying to make something out of the land they live on, without the knowledge necessary to achieve these goals. There is a sense in which they are never settled in *ur*, a housing estate that does not belong to them in any tangible way. The earth rebels against their efforts to tame it and all their schemes fall short of their expectations. In this respect, the novel mirrors essentially untenable European efforts to farm Australian land.

Blueprints for a Barbed-Wire Canoe has been described as being reminiscent of Elizabeth Jolley's *The Well*, due to its all-pervading sense

---

5 Rundle, http://members.dodo.com.au/~ghannah/macauleybfabwc.html.

of entrapment and enclosure. *The Well* is centred around a well in which a person has purportedly fallen. Similarly, much of the action in *Blueprints for a Barbed-Wire Canoe* is focused on the wall that surrounds the estate. Built to keep vandals at bay, the wall also serves to alienate the residents further from the rest of the country. They are effectively walled in their own ghetto where they slowly starve due to their lack of supplies. The wall may be seen as a reflection on Australia's insular attitude that effectively cuts it off from potentially fruitful outside influences.

Mythical underpinnings

Blueprints for a Barbed-Wire Canoe might be described as a modern-day myth. It models itself on a number of more distant myths, yet its location is distinctly contemporary. In particular, the novel contains elements of the myth of Abraham, the myth of Ur, the Epic of Gilgamesh, and the Song of Solomon; yet it is more than a mere composite. Macauley uses these ancient stories as starting points for his own suburban tale.

Ur of the Chaldees

The lines which preface the novel come from an ancient Sumerian poem. The city of Ur which is mentioned in the poem refers to one of the first civilisations, called 'Ur of the Chaldees', which was founded in the area now known as Iraq, and its name derives from the first city-state, Uruk. As Guy Rundle points out, there is a significant amount of poetry still in existence from this era that features people going to taverns and festivals, as well as people staying at home and feeling alone. Rundle suggests that

> in six thousand years of urban habitation, nothing has really changed … the stories that you read in the epic poems of those early cities are about the same sort of people that we are.[6]

---

6 Rundle, http://members.dodo.com.au/~ghannah/macauleybfabwc.html.

Abraham

Bram may take his name from Abraham, the founder of Judaism, who came from the city of Ur. Abraham is recognised by Christians and is also a very important prophet in Islam. The story of his life is told in the Biblical Book of Genesis and in the Koran. His original name was Abram, which was succeeded later in life by the name Abraham. In Islam, Abraham (or Ibrahim) is considered one of the first and most important prophets, and is commonly called Khalil Ullah, 'Friend of God'. There is no contemporary mention of his life, and no source earlier than his mention in Genesis, so it is difficult to know whether he was a real historical figure. If he was, he probably lived between 2166 B.C. and 1991 B.C.

The account of Abraham's life found in the Book of Genesis begins in Chapter 11, at the close of a genealogy of the sons of Shem. Abraham is said to have lived in 'Ur of the Chaldees', which was an important centre of Sumerian culture and an ancient Mesopotamian city. Its ruins are approximately midway between the modern city of Baghdad, Iraq, and the head of the Persian Gulf, south of the Euphrates River, on the edge of the Al Hajarah Desert. The site of Ur is known today as Tall al Muqayyar, Iraq. In antiquity, the Euphrates River flowed near the city walls. Controlling this outlet to the sea, Ur was favorably located for the development of commerce and for attaining political dominance.

Archaeological excavations have indicated that in Abraham's day the inhabitants of Ur worshipped idols like the Moon God, Nannar. This may account for the name of 'Nanna', the old lady who runs a flower shop in Macauley's *ur*. While she is not an object of worship in the estate, her death is a significant turning point for the other residents because her life is sacrificed in the name of progress. Everyone recognises the injustice and stupidity of her violent demise, which causes them to resist even more fiercely the construction of the freeway.

The Book of Genesis recounts that when Abraham saw his city attacked by hosts of enemies from the north and from the low-lying lands to the south, there was nothing left for him to do but migrate to the country that

God promised to give him. In Macauley's story, Bram decides to move to another estate once his enemies have destroyed *ur* and his history is finally written.

Different reasons are given for the ultimate demise of the historical Ur – some sources claim that it was destroyed by a flood, while others say that it was the re-routing of the Euphrates which sealed its fate. In *Blueprints for a Barbed-Wire Canoe*, rains flood the area towards the end of Bram's solitary habitation there, which may be a link to the decline of the real Ur. Alternatively, we might see *ur*'s fate as being decided at the very beginning when the freeway is not built as promised. Bram makes a direct comparison between the promised freeway and a river which delivers sustenance: 'We ... lived like dry stones scattered under an unforgiving sky, we had no mighty river of a freeway to irrigate us, to give us cars and life' (p.18).

GENRE, STRUCTURE & STYLE

Structure

Blueprints for a Barbed-Wire Canoe is divided into fifteen numbered but untitled chapters that are narrated by the main character, Bram. It has an unusual structure because it begins with a dramatic event that happens towards the end of the story, when the settlement of *ur* has been almost completely destroyed. The reader does not fully realise the significance of this tragedy until they have reached the later portions of the novel. Since the climax is given away so early, the author is able to give the novel another ending, which ties up all the loose ends.

The role of conversations

Often the significance of the novel's action is explored through long conversations, like the ones between Bram and Michael and Bram and Alex. These long discussions also serve to enhance character development. Bram begins to understand Michael's motivations when he goes to ask him to help build a rabbit fence. Once he hears Michael's life story Bram is able to make more sense of Michael's strange behaviour (pp.26–30). There is one very long speech by the government official, Loch, which reveals the duplicity of the authorities in relation to *ur* (pp.74–82). Similarly, Bram's conversation with Alex at the rubbish tip is an important turning point in his evolution as a character. He finally sees the ruin that the estate has become and feels nauseous in response, overwhelmed by the degradation he and the others have endured (p.47).

Narrative style

We see *ur* through Bram's viewpoint and witness his journey from hope to despair and back again. His frame of mind shifts significantly throughout the telling of his tale. Sometimes he is optimistic and social, at others he is depressed and withdrawn. Bram sifts through dirt looking for objects which will make the story of *ur* complete. However, there is

always a piece missing – the absent Jodie. He reconstructs recent history in the manner of an archaeologist studying an ancient civilisation. His neighbours and friends, who are now lost, have all left their traces upon the objects they have touched. This estate has aged beyond its years in an accelerated process of decay, rendering it a garbage heap to be trawled through by Bram – who is referred to by Michael as the "resident intellectual" (p.55).

Blueprints for a Barbed-Wire Canoe is a novel which experiments with style. It is a novel which subtly reflects on its own process through the narrator's remarks about his obsessive quest to reconstruct the past. He explains that he fills the gaps in the narrative – the unknowable aspects – with fiction and fantasy. At the same time, he worries about telling the story on behalf of other people and the inevitable distortion of truth that this process entails. We are reading the story he tells at the same time as he is struggling to write it down. As a narrator, Bram is emotional and detached by turns. At times he withdraws from the chaos of *ur*'s destruction, which makes him unable to recount events, except by cobbling together bits of hearsay from the other residents. Even though he was present in *ur* during most of its history, he must still perform an act of excavation to understand what really happened.

In chapter 14, Bram expresses his anxiety about the writing process and the difficulty of fitting all the necessary pieces together into a coherent narrative. The ghost of his father helps him through this period of uncertainty, delivering a sense of purpose. Part of the reason he stays behind amid the ruins of *ur* is to commune with the ghosts of the dead and sift through the debris that has been left behind. He reflects on the writing of the story we are reading, drawing attention to the painful process involved.

Allegorical fable

Traditionally, fables are understood as fictitious narratives based on myths or legends which are intended to convey a moral. The fable is one of the oldest literary forms – much older than the novel or the short story.

A fable is usually short, written in either verse or prose, and conveys a clear moral or message. The earliest fables still preserved date back to sixth century Greece B.C. The author of these fables, Aesop, used animal characters to stand for human 'types'. Although Aesop's fables are ostensibly about animals, they are really instructional tales about human emotions and behaviour.

Most fables have at least two levels of meaning. On the surface, the fable may be about animals. But on a second level, the animals stand for kinds of people or ideas. The way the animals interact and the way the plot unfolds convey something about the nature of people or the value of ideas. Any type of fiction that has multiple levels of meaning in this way is called an 'allegory'.

Blueprints for a Barbed-Wire Canoe can be described as an allegorical fable because it operates on a number of levels. On the surface level, the story about the inhabitants of a failed housing estate is very moving, if sometimes implausible. While the setting of the story in a failed housing estate is fairly plausible, some of the events which unfold require the reader to suspend their disbelief. At the same time, each of the characters might be read as symbols for various aspects of Australian culture. For instance, Vito and Marie-Claire are European migrants who struggle to make themselves at home in a hostile environment. The speeches given by the representatives of local government, Leyland and Loch, symbolise the treachery of bureaucrats working on behalf of the government. As a character, Slug may represent the human tendency for treacherous behaviour, because he crosses over from being a resident to an enemy of *ur*.

On another level, the novel is concerned with the deceptions perpetrated by powerful organisations. The narrative serves to warn us about the possible consequences of overdeveloping the Australian landscape in the name of profit. By inventing a bleak scenario of isolated individuals living in squalor on the outskirts of Melbourne, Macauley critiques the current tendency for seemingly endless outward expansion. As Bronwyn Rivers observes, the story is 'perhaps intended as a salutary fable about the horrors awaiting our disaffected modern citizenry: these

isolated urban dwellers, abandoned by government and their fellow citizens, descend into wildness'.[7] Another way of looking at the novel is to see the estate and its social context as a microcosm of contemporary Australian society, with the various characters representing forces at work in our community, especially the tension between the powerful and the underprivileged. *Blueprints for a Barbed-Wire Canoe* may be seen as a highly political novel about the Australian social landscape, even though it does not immediately appear that way.

Many aspects of the narrative serve to puncture the illusion that it is a realistic novel, reminding the reader that it can also be read as an allegorical fable. While the basic narrative may be almost believable at the beginning, the plot is stretched to the level of farce. The central motif of the barbed-wire canoe is a fanciful idea, invented by Jodie's great grandfather: obviously it would be an impossible folly to navigate a river in a canoe made of barbed wire. Other aspects of the novel also seem far-fetched, like the qauntity of parcels that are dropped from planes. Intended as forms of assistance, these parcels fall so frequently that they become dangerous missiles, eventually killing Dave when one falls on his head. Nanna's death, caused by a bulldozer running over her, is similarly implausible – yet her sacrifice performs a symbolic function, showing that the authorities will stop at nothing to achieve their goals. The endless blunders of local government officials reinforce the idea that bureaucracy works against ordinary people, ruining their lives in order to carry out their ill-considered plans.

Macauley has said that he was attracted to depicting this outer suburban landscape 'because it is precisely that state of in-between-ness, that strange marginality, that neither rural nor quite yet urban landscape, a place of hope, dream, possibility, that became in my mind a metaphor for who we actually are'.[8] This location provided him with a backdrop for

7 Rivers, Bronwyn 'A descent into the wildness of isolation', Sydney Morning Herald, 5–6 June 2004, http://members.dodo.com.au/~ghannah/macauleybfabwc.html#The_Sydney_Morning_Herald_Review.

8 Macauley, 'Where do I come from?', http://members.dodo.com.au/~ghannah/macauley.html.

expressing his criticisms of the myths we live by in the so-called 'lucky country'. Through this allegorical fable he tries to show how European attempts to 'tame the landscape', 'fence it up' and create dream lives are doomed to failure because this involves the erasure of our bloody history.[9] .

9 Macauley, 'Where do I come from?', http://members.dodo.com.au/~ghannah/macauley.html.

CHAPTER–BY–CHAPTER ANALYSIS

Chapter 1 (pp.1–5)

Summary: *The narrator hears of Jodie's death; he begins writing an account of life in the estate.*

The novel begins with its end. There is a description of the prolonged, heavy rain which falls for three days, flooding the local creek. A young woman has drowned after unsuccessfully launching a barbed-wire canoe, while dressed in a uniform and rabbit skin hat. Bram, the narrator, is asked to identify the body and sign some papers after this incident. The rain continues washing everything clean'. The rain has a cleansing effect, washing away a 'sad sorry story' (p.2), making the narrator conclude that his time in this place is over.

Over the course of an evening, Bram drinks beer and tries to write a letter breaking the news to Michael. Leaving his house, Bram stands at the top of a mountain of rubble, remembering happier times. The entire housing estate, which was once bustling with people, is now drenched by grey water and mud. Scratched by the weeds which have taken over the streets, Bram notices how ruined the neighbourhood has become. The nature of the narrator's surroundings mirrors his sense of desolation. He returns home and surrounds himself with relics, urging them to help tell his story. Bram wakes in the night with the image of Jodie's lifeless body before him once again. He reveals that she was pregnant before she died, but the newborn baby was not with her when she was found. Determined to stay one more night, he builds a makeshift dyke to keep floodwaters at bay. He describes himself as the only witness to the final act of the failed estate, the 'last spectator in an empty theatre' (p.5). As the only person left, he feels a responsibility to put his experiences on paper, as testimony to the existence of a once-thriving community.

Q How does the narrator's decision to stay alone in the ruined estate reflect on his character?

Chapter 2 (pp.6–15)

Summary: *The estate is officially opened; sewerage problems emerge; the northern housing project is forgotten in favour of the east.*

The story that the narrator has written begins in this chapter. He describes his decision to buy into the estate as a 'mistake from the first' (p.6). Like his neighbours, he was a 'victim of the publicity' (p.6) that sold the estate as a desirable location in comparison with overcrowded cities. With hindsight, the narrator believes that the urban developers who designed the estate looked '*too far out*' and '*in the wrong direction*' (pp.6–7). The land that the estate is built on is described as 'forty hectares of overworked and abandoned farmland' full of 'rabbit holes' and 'Scotch thistle' (p.7). Despite the shoddy job done by the designers and builders, the opening of the estate is attended by many dignitaries, including the Premier.

The sewerage system is soon discovered to be faulty: it emits an unpleasant odour. The petrol station hasn't been built and none of the phones work. These early signs prompt people to try to sell their properties, realising that they have made an error of judgment. Weeds begin to take over, giving parts of the estate a wild, scruffy appearance. Nature starts to invade the architecture: birds' nests make roofs sag and floodwaters undermine foundations. The number of residents begins to dwindle as the conditions worsen while the bonds between the remaining residents tighten. At this point, most residents are forced to acknowledge that the developers made a terrible mistake building houses in inhospitable country to the north of Melbourne.

Meanwhile, another estate springs up to the east, causing the government to overlook the plight of the original northern community. The northern freeway plan is discarded in favour of an eastern freeway, leaving the estate to its fate. At the end of the chapter, the narrator claims that the 'original dream was shattered' and 'all but the deluded had fled' (p.14). The estate becomes depopulated and ghost-infested, a 'testament for any visitor ... to some now very anonymous architect's grand but

misguided vision' (p.15). Becoming more isolated, the people living there become increasingly self-sufficient out of necessity. A new community is born out of the chaos and detritus of the failed estate.

Q What compensations emerge from the failure of the estate to fulfil its planned potential?

Chapter 3 (pp.16–24)

Summary: *The residents pool their money. They begin money-making schemes including market gardening, rabbit shooting, beer brewing, flower selling and scavenging. Bonds are formed between people over beer at Slug and Dave's bar.*

Bram sees the nights spent drinking under the stars with his fellow residents as the 'real beginning' (p.16) – the moment when a community is born. For him, the history of the estate and its demise is merely a pre-history, or a prelude to the real action which happened between people living there.

Initially he uses his role as the newspaper editor to publish inflammatory articles about the neglect of estate residents by the state government. This position gives him a degree of authority in the eyes of his neighbours, even though his paper, *The Voice,* eventually ceases production as the population decreases.

Vito takes the initiative and starts using the sewerage overflow as fertiliser for his garden, growing enough produce to sell in the world outside and providing the community with petty cash. After this, the residents decide to pool their money and make joint decisions about how best to spend it. Prompted by Vito's action, Nanna sells flowers on the highway every weekend and Craig, the squatter, sells scavenged parts from deserted houses. Dave brews beer; Slug buys a trailer, pump and generator; Michael shoots rabbits. They sell their cars, which are useless without a freeway, and contribute the profits to the common fund. In this way they create a communal economy based on sharing rather than individualism. Slug and Dave set up a bar where everybody can drink in

the evenings, which becomes the social hub of the estate. This growing bond between people makes them feel a greater connection with the land around. Once the original boundaries have been broken down, they use their resources in innovative ways.

Q What does the decision by remaining residents to pool their money say about their new way of life?

Chapter 4 (pp.25–32)

Summary: *The origins of the name given to the estate are explained. Bram sees Michael building something out of barbed wire and hears his life story; vandals break in and desecrate parts of the estate. Craig declares his love for Marie-Claire; Michael begins armed sentry duty at night.*

By renaming the *Outer Suburban Village Development Complex 'ur'*, the residents reinvent the place for themselves, erasing previous connotations. Bram reflects on the fact that the estate does not exist for the rest of the world, because it has been erased from cartographers' maps. The residents receive occasional visits from outsiders wishing to join them, who leave as soon as they smell the sewage, reinforcing their sense of isolation and uniqueness. Bram spends his days writing articles for his newspaper and going over the estate accounts. One day he approaches Michael to ask if he will help build fences to keep rabbits out of Vito's garden and discovers that he is building something out of timber and barbed wire in his garage which he will not discuss. They talk long into the night and Bram learns about Michael's tragic past: his fencing accident, which left him partially sighted, his marriage break-up and his estrangement from his daughter. By helping the others with the construction of a garden fence, Michael becomes properly inducted into the community, instead of being on its margins.

Vandals break in and ruin the phone box, which is the estate's only real link to the outside world. This disturbs Craig, who has begun a long-distance relationship with a Frenchwoman named Marie-Claire. The others allow him to use the car to ring her from a phone box in the

nearest town, thereby acknowledging his insider status. In response to the attacks of vandalism, Michael stands guard every night with his rifle, despite Bram's misgivings:

> Soon I stopped trying to talk sense into him, he would not listen anyway, and I along with the others came to accept the sight of him standing out there as part of our daily lives. (p.32)

Q How do visits from the outside world unsettle *ur's* residents?

Chapter 5 (pp.33–9)

Summary: *Winter sets in. Michael's daughter, Jodie, arrives; Bram falls in love with her. He asks her about what Michael is building and she tells him about the plans for the barbed-wire canoe.*

Winter confines the residents' movements, so they prefer to stay indoors. Michael's daughter, Jodie, arrives without any announcement. After fighting for a few nights, father and daughter settle into a domestic routine. This induces twinges of jealousy in the others who have left their own families behind.

Bram is reminded that the community he is part of 'is an ersatz family compared to the one linked by blood' (pp.34–5). Jodie's presence turns winter into a 'kind of spring' (p.35) for the others – she ushers in a whole new phase of activity to improve the estate.

Jodie's arrival makes Bram realise how lonely and isolated he has become: 'It's an unguarded stairway ... from the warm house of solitude to the dungeon of loneliness and I had without knowing begun to descend it' (p.36). He invites her to dinner and questions her about what her father is building in his garage. She says that it is a kind of 'running joke in the family' (p.36) which has been passed down from her great-grandfather who fought in the Boer war. Members of each generation inherit the plans to launch a barbed-wire canoe before they die. The ever-optimistic Bram describes this as a form of 'inherited pessimism' (p.38) which Michael tried to put behind him when he moved to the estate. Regarding him with 'the look of the doubter in her eye' (p.38), Jodie finds it hard to

understand Bram's endless hopefulness in the face of the estate's obvious decay. He dismisses her story about the canoe, thinking it a fiction, and loving her all the more for her inventiveness.

Q What effect does Jodie's presence have on the mood of the residents?

Chapter 6 (pp40–8)

Summary: *The weather becomes warmer. Rubbish is repeatedly dumped at the edge of the estate; Bram makes friends with Alex, the tip attendant. Bram begins to see the estate as a 'grotesquerie' (p.46).*

The residents notice clouds of dust as a road is built nearby, and then witness the dumping of rubbish. Bram writes a letter of complaint to the government department responsible and receives an apology, but the tip remains. This sudden brush with bureaucracy leaves the residents feeling detached and exhausted. They accept the tip's presence, as they have all their other misfortunes: 'the tip had become part of our lives; we soon forgot how, why, or even when, and accepted the fact as given' (p.42). Bram begins to understand that they are 'living *wrongly*' and 'pretending it [is] right': 'no amount of adaptation could ever compensate for the fact that the basic idea was wrong' (p.43). His love for Jodie makes him think seriously of leaving to make a better life for himself.

One hot night, Bram ventures out to the tip and talks to Alex, the tip attendant, who also happens to be Nanna's son. Alex acknowledges that the government considers *ur* to be a 'blot on the landscape' which needs to be removed (p.46). This comment leads Bram to view the estate through an outsider's eyes: '*ur* had become a grotesquerie, and the most grotesque part about it was that we who lived here couldn't see it' (p.46). After a night of drinking with Alex, Bram feels 'the will to go on drain completely' (p.47). The estate suddenly fills him with revulsion, making him violently ill. This is an important turning point for the formerly optimistic narrator.

Q What is the significance of Bram's uncontrollable bout of retching?

Chapter 7 (pp.49–61)

Summary: *The vandals return; Michael builds a wall. Slug departs; cows wander into the Square. Marie-Claire arrives from France; the estate savings disappear; Layland, a government official, arrives with a message.*

The vandals return and almost demolish Slug's bar with Alex's bulldozer. This leads to a discussion of the role of the estate in relation to the outside world. In conversation with Michael, Bram puts forward the idea that the vandals aren't vandals at all: that they are, in fact, working for the government. In his view, the government introduced the tip as 'a calculated move' to get rid of the estate (p.50). Michael asks why Bram is telling him all this, suggesting that it's because Bram is in love with his daughter. Michael begins building a wall to keep out further attacks, using bricks from abandoned houses, barbed wire and bottles. The enclosing of the estate forces Bram to move closer to the others, reinforcing his sense of inclusion.

A series of unusual events generates a sense of foreboding. Slug's bar is vandalised then he leaves unexpectedly, cows break into the Square and the estate savings account disappears. For Bram, Marie-Claire's arrival from France reinforces the weirdness of their way of life: 'I watched the frivolity surrounding Marie-Claire's arrival as one who is already drifting away' (p.53–4).

Bram's gloomy presentiments are confirmed when Layland arrives with the message that the government is preparing to demolish *ur* to build a freeway for another estate in the north-west. This new development forces Bram to stay despite his desire to flee. However, his sense of unease grows as he surveys his changed surroundings: 'The bulldozer looked like some strange enormous animal jaw open, teeth bared, waiting to strike. What days ahead!' (p.61).

Q How does Bram interpret the series of unexplained events?

Chapter 8 (pp.62–71)

Summary: *Layland tries to escape and Michael shoots him in the leg; the power and water are disconnected; Craig accidentally loses the last of their money; food supplies drop from the sky.*

Ur assumes a siege mentality. Nobody arrives or leaves for 223 days. The wall stands as a symbol of the increasing ghettoisation of the community. While it was built to protect them, it also serves to keep them trapped inside in ever-worsening conditions:

> The wall might be a protection against the vandals and any other form of violent assault but it could do nothing to stop the slow rot that was now eating us away from the inside. (p.67)

Here Bram expresses his concern for the wellbeing of the community, which is slowly decaying under pressure from outside forces.

Bram tells Layland that he is welcome to stay as long as he needs to, because the residents of *ur* are hospitable people: 'On the outside … we might look like a hard-bitten bunch but you would never find us throwing a guest out on the street' (p.63). Michael decides, on behalf of the others, that they will not accept the government's offer to relocate them. The residents worry about the consequences of this decision but they do not disagree. Michael behaves angrily towards Layland. This makes Layland try to escape but Michael shoots him and he is again unable to move. Once a good talker, Layland retreats into silence, relying on notes to communicate his needs. The power is cut, leaving them in darkness and without refrigeration. Then the water is turned off, forcing them to rely on rainwater.

Layland's leg becomes infected and Craig attempts to drive out of *ur* to get supplies, but he is thwarted by the lack of access to the highway and loses the last of their money in the process. They are reduced to scavenging from the tip and slaughtering cows for food until supplies begin to drop from the sky. Bram invites Jodie over to share a food parcel together and tells her he loves her. She responds ambiguously with an expression that could be read as a grimace or a smile.

Q What does the wall symbolise for those inside the estate?

Chapter 9 (pp72–84)

Summary: *Loch and two other officials arrive with a proposition. Layland's leg is amputated; guards are provided for the estate.*

Bram compares the arrival of the official visitors with the 'sweet perfume of a bunch of flowers' (p.72) after the community's extended isolation. Loch, a man in a suit from an unidentified government department, accompanied by two blue-uniformed men, addresses the residents. He sees that their 'sweet little piece of suburban paradise' has become an 'inglorious shambles' (p.72). Loch visits Layland, whose leg has been amputated by Marie-Claire due to the onset of gangrene. Bram catches Jodie's eye during the meeting with Loch and realises that she judges him harshly for his former optimism.

Loch makes a number of statements about how the estate has been forgotten – a situation which he hopes to remedy. He claims that Layland's message was erroneous, that in fact the government had no intention of building other estates so far out, describing the the *Outer Suburban Village Development Complex* as a 'joke' (p.78). Loch sets out a significant shift in the government's planning philosophy:

> We simply cannot afford to think along these lines any more: expansion and more expansion, a continual 'looking out,' the idea that every inch of empty space should be considered useless unless filled has lost all popularity now and rightly so. (p.78)

He declares that the estate 'was doomed to failure from the start' (p.78), a mistake which still needs to be fixed, and he tries to persuade the residents to trust him. Offering protection and compensation for the wrongs done to them, as well as food supplies, Loch appears genuine. Michael suspiciously takes notes and makes Loch sign them, which he does reluctantly. When they discover that the boxes of 'supplies' are full of old rubbish, they are less convinced of the truthfulness of his speech.

Q What effect does Loch's speech have on the atmosphere of *ur*?

KEY POINT

This chapter reveals one of the main themes of the novel: the duplicitous nature of bureaucracy and the harm it can do to ordinary people.

Chapter 10 (pp.85–97)

Summary: *Bram promises to lock himself inside for good; Vito leaves for Melbourne; Craig begins to dismantle the wall; Michael threatens him with a gun; residents see a road being built; Nanna is accidentally killed by a bulldozer.*

Bram is sick of everything so he declares that he is going to stay inside from now on. However, Jodie soon manages to coax him out of his reclusion. Vito disappears during the night and no-one knows why. Craig and Marie-Claire begin to dismantle the wall, in accordance with the promise the residents have made to Loch. Michael threatens them with a gun, asserting his dominance over everyone, including the two guards, who flee in terror. Dave tries to intervene, then runs out into the paddocks, only to discover that a road is being constructed and is coming towards them. Michael comes up with the idea of building a moat around *ur* using the bulldozer. The men begin using guerrilla tactics to sabotage the construction of the road, blowing up 'three bulldozers, two graders and a roller' in one night (p.90).

This 'triumph' is not, however, celebrated by Bram, who spends the night in the bucket of the bulldozer with Jodie (p.90). Remembering this blissful night later, he understands that the end for *ur* is near. This period of intimacy seems to heighten Bram's perceptions of the situation he and the others are in. Slug reappears as a representative of the council and tries to dissuade them from continuing with their current course of action, but his words are with cynicism. Nobody believes what he has to say because they have been told lies for too long. Michael shoots at him and drives him away. In protest at the threat to their homes, Nanna sits in front of an enormous bulldozer and, in the confusion, is crushed by it when the driver makes an error.

This tragic event sparks a chain reaction involving people from outside the estate who protest on their behalf. The residents are literally bombarded by food parcels which provide a brief respite from the ongoing siege. They retreat into their own worlds: Dave stays in front of

his old bar thinking of Slug; Alex disappears inside after the death of his mother; Bram and Jodie spend more time alone together. Bram's love for Jodie causes him to dream that the situation has been transformed – he longs to have a quiet suburban life instead being caught in the violent reality that surrounds him.

Q Why do the residents retreat into their own worlds when faced with the threat of demolition?

Chapter 11 (pp98–106)

Summary: *Dave is killed by a falling parcel; Michael acts insanely; Bram realises that Michael is mad when he gives Bram the blueprints for a barbed-wire canoe.*

Michael continues to roam around the edges of the estate, guarding it against real and imagined threats. Alex remains out of sight while Dave seems to be stuck in the past, behaving like a bartender although there are no customers. Jodie warns Dave that he is endangering himself by remaining in the Square, but he is killed by a falling food parcel before anybody can talk him into moving inside. Ironically it is a gift, rather than enemy aggression, that kills him. Dave is buried next to the inauguration plaque as a reminder of the failure of the much-lauded housing project.

Dave's death incenses Michael, who fires at anything associated with 'the murderers' (p.98). After endless rounds of ammunition are spent, he asks to speak to Bram and Jodie. He tells them that he approves of their relationship, which embarrasses Jodie. Michael reveals his plan to save the two young couples from outsiders, so they can marry and raise a new generation. Bram sees that 'Michael was mad, had already led us into the most inexplicable madnesses and was about to take us even further' (p.102). Bram realises that he and the other residents have entrusted their futures to an insane man, because they haven't had the strength to fight his influence. Upon leaving, Michael gives Bram the blueprints for the barbed-wire canoe which Bram reads in the middle of the night. The instructions are absurd and poignant: an expression of defiance in the face of life's inevitable cycles of growth and decay, of births and deaths.

Q How does Michael's speech alter Bram's understanding of *ur's* desperate situation?

Chapter 12 (pp.107–18)

Summary: *Alex leaves* ur *in the night, driving the bulldozer through the wall. Slug returns with a warning; Craig and Michael embark on a 'final stand' (p.113) as* ur *is destroyed. The others move to the nearest town for shelter; Bram experiences a happy suburban fantasy; Jodie leaves with the blueprints.*

Michael decides to demolish the remaining houses and use the debris to bolster the weakened wall. Alex thwarts this project by leaving in the night, demolishing part of the wall with his bulldozer on the way. Craig and Michael try to repair the wall but it is as fragile as 'a house of cards' (p.108). The others realise that the road will soon break through *ur*'s fortifications and they prepare to escape. Bram perceives that Craig has become 'infected' with Michael's madness, and finds it difficult to look him in the eye (p.108). He reflects on the irony of Michael's suburban dream of the two couples living side by side, when they are in the midst of a battle zone.

Slug returns to try to help them after being pricked by his conscience. Bram has to convey the news about Dave and Nanna's deaths, which Slug takes badly, insisting on seeing Dave's grave. After being complicit in the demolition of *ur,* Slug now wishes to help the survivors, offering them shelter in a local pub for the night. Craig begs for petrol from Slug's tank to make bottle bombs as weapons for the final confrontation with the road workers. At the pub, Bram and Jodie drink champagne and consummate their love in a room smelling of mothballs.

That night, Michael and Craig prepare to make their final assault on horseback. Craig flees after things go wrong, suddenly aware of the foolhardiness of further resistance. He and Marie-Claire reunite at the pub, then head for the airport to leave immediately for France. Bram gets up in the night and comes across a cleaner named Tony, who originally worked on the estate as a builder. This man is still harbouring a dream

of building more houses, even though he knows his building days are probably over. Seeing this kind of optimism in somebody else makes Bram realise how deluded he has been. Nevertheless, he indulges in a fantasy of domestic bliss with Jodie; a fantasy that is shattered when he returns to the room and discovers that she has left with the blueprints.

Q What does Bram's conversation with Tony tell us about the propensity of human beings to keep on hoping in the face of failure?

Chapter 13 (pp.119–29)

Summary: Ur *is partly bulldozed; Michael and Jodie become outlaws and rumours circulate about their activities; Bram publicly disavows any connection with them.*

Living at the pub, Bram hears rumours about the activities of Michael and Jodie but is unable to confirm them. Through secondhand scraps of information he pieces together a picture of their days on the run after the destruction of *ur*. He is no longer able to ask them what really happened, so he must construct his own narrative about their exploits.

Michael's last act at *ur* is to build a small fence around Dave's grave to protect it from the bulldozers. In this way, he tries to honour the dead of *ur* and emphasise the sacrifices they have made in its defence. According to reports, Michael becomes a fugitive destroying anything connected with the government, shire council or housing in general. Unbeknown to him, he has attracted a following of disgruntled farmers who believe that he shares their grievances. A competing story begins to gain popularity. This claims that Michael is in fact protesting against the mistreatment of housing estates, which makes him unpopular with the farmers, his former supporters. But a new group of supporters emerge who admire his stand against the injustice perpetrated by local government. He also becomes an embarrassment to the police, who are desperate to apprehend him.

One night, Patterson, the old police sergeant, takes Bram aside and warns that Michael is going to be trapped in a faked housing estate. He asks Bram to warn Michael to lie low and keep out of trouble until it all blows over. This prompts Bram to declare that he has no allegiance to

Michael, despite all rumours. Afterwards, he is shunned by people who thought he was a friend of the famous outlaw, and this declaration ends his involvement in the 'Michael affair' (p.128). Michael is captured, but Jodie disappears. There are many stories about where she is but none of them are completely convincing.

Q What role does rumour play in Bram's reconstruction of the 'Michael affair'?

Chapter 14 (pp.130–40)

Summary: *Bram returns to live at* ur*; he begins writing a history of the estate.*

Bram decides to leave the pub; he and Alex return to *ur* for a visit. Once there, Bram is convinced that he must move back. Tony, the bricklayer, helps him build a shack out of the debris left from the road construction, which has been brought to a stop halfway through. Tony continues to visit Bram once a week until he leaves for another satellite town to find work.

Bram feels a moment of jealousy when a postcard arrives from Craig and Marie-Claire, who are holidaying in her hometown of Ur in France. He remembers that he and Jodie were the other young couple in the estate, and now Jodie is gone. This leads him to think about the oddity of human existence: 'How strange and ravelled our lives can be!' (p.136).

He reflects on his desire to see Jodie, realising that he has returned so she can find him again:

> each morning I stood on top of the hill and scanned the horizon in the hope of catching a glimpse of Jodie, returning at last to the home I'd built for us out of the ruins of the past. (p.134)

Bram is caught between past and future in a 'speculative half-lived present' (p.136). Recognising that most of his life in *ur* has been distinguished by hope for brighter possibilities, he awaits Jodie's arrival.

Without Jodie and their unborn child, Bram is doomed to dwelling exclusively in the past. Sifting through the ruins of *ur* he finds long-lost

> "When I first mentioned the wall to Bram he didn't try to stop me ... it wasn't until some time after that I realised why: he was nodding his head out of love." (p.101)

In other words, love softens Bram and clouds his judgment.

Jodie also has the ability to sway him from firm decisions. At one point, he declares that he is going to lock himself in his house for good, but this doesn't last. Jodie draws him out again, to face the conflict between the residents and the road-workers (p.85).

On a number of occasions, Bram decides to leave *ur* but cannot bring himself to do it. When he goes into town to withdraw money from the estate's savings account he plans to start a new life with Jodie using the proceeds. Then he discovers that the account has been closed by the authorities and his hopes are dashed once more (p.54). It is difficult to tell whether Bram's failure to leave *ur* is due more to weakness of character or to a sense of loyalty.

Bram feels conflicting emotions when he discovers that Jodie has left him in favour of accompanying her father on a tour of destruction. He feels anger towards Michael for taking Jodie away on a foolhardy escapade. He continues to hope for her return after she disappears, knowing on some level that he is deluded to do so. In response, he retreats to his own company as a way of coping with his loss and making sense of the tragedy of *ur*.

He finds most satisfaction in piecing together the story of the estate after its dissolution. When his writing is going well, he is exhilarated by the process of creating a coherent narrative explaining how the estate came to be destroyed. He sees himself as the last remaining witness, with a responsibility to produce a text that honours the departed and dead.

An optimist at heart, Bram tends to believe that something better will occur in the near future, even when the worst has happened. The last lines of the novel indicate that he intends to start again by putting his obsession with the past behind him: 'that nonsense is over ... tomorrow I leave for Haranhope where a barrow of bricks lies waiting' (p.147). The image of bricks waiting for him indicates that he has not completely given up on the idea of literally building a decent life for himself elsewhere. Like that

of Tony the 'deluded' (p.118) bricklayer, Bram's sense of hope is resilient and life-affirming.

Q In what way does Bram's bout of nausea reflect his state of mind?

Bram's relationship with Jodie

Key Quotes

'Jodie I love you, I said. Her lips turned up into a grimace or a smile, I still don't know which, and she turned and walked out into the dark.' (p.71)
'I looked up for a moment and caught Jodie's eye, the briefest glance; there was no sympathy, no forgiveness in it.' (p.73)
'I fell asleep in the bucket that night with Jodie in my arms. Never have I felt such warmth, such bliss.' (p.90)

We never gain a sense that Jodie really cares for Bram. There is physical intimacy and a kind of understanding between them, but we don't hear her side of the relationship, so her thoughts remain mysterious. She comes across as a strong woman who can judge other people harshly on occasion. For instance, she is scathing about Bram's optimistic nature, seeing this as a character flaw rather than a positive trait. By contrast, she is extremely loyal to her father, no matter what he does. In the end, her loyalty to Michael brings about her downfall. Instead of choosing a family life with Bram she aligns herself with the past, perhaps trying to make amends for her rocky relationship with her father. All he can provide her with is his own madness and an inherited death wish, while Bram offers his devotion. Given her life story, we may surmise that she is more at ease with chaos than with harmony and chooses this option accordingly.

It may be argued that gender roles are reversed to a certain extent in Bram and Jodie's relationship. He likes being at home and desires a secure future in a stable, loving relationship, while she seems more interested in being an outlaw and has little concern for the consequences. He is the one who is lovelorn and needy, whereas we are not given any insight into Jodie's emotions.

objects which help him to reconstruct the estate's history in words. His dream of domestic bliss fades and is replaced by an obsessive desire to write down everything about *ur* and its destruction. Bram dreams of his father bent over with a swag full of barbed wire and broken wood, wheezing heavily and whistling. His father says he is going 'Down to the creek' (p.140), which fills Bram with a feeling of warmth and purpose. Suddenly he accepts the fact that his lonely days in *ur* have 'only just begun' (p.140).

Q What does Bram's dream about his father signify?

Chapter 15 (pp.141–7)

Summary: *Bram identifies Jodie's body at the morgue and tries to reconstruct her last hours. He leaves for a new job in another satellite town as the freeway construction resumes.*

After Jodie's death, Bram understands that she was the piece missing from his story. He brings a lock of her hair home from the morgue and adds it to his collection of relics. He finds satisfaction in finally understanding what has happened to *ur*. Patterson, the police chief, brings the remains of the barbed-wire canoe and the rabbit skin hat worn first by Michael and then inherited by Jodie. Bram finally broaches the last part of the narrative concerning Jodie's final adventure in the creek. Once this is done, he buries all the junk he had previously unearthed. He is slow-moving and heavy with unacknowledged grief.

On the horizon Bram sees the bulldozers starting up, as construction of the freeway resumes again, turning it in another direction. Bram muses that in the future *ur* will only be remembered as a 'dangerous bend' (p.146) on the road to the new estate in the west. Patterson helps Bram tow his car from the bog so he is able to leave before they reach him. He packs his things, continuing to reflect on the past and 'the sometimes silly things that happen in this life and that so soon pass into the obscurity of history' (p.147). Leaving *ur* means a new start for Bram, an end to his

days of nostalgia and recollection. In the future he plans to become a man of action rather than reflection, and to 'start from the bottom up' (p.147).

Q What does Bram mean when he says that he won't be 'setting sail' on his papers (p.147)?

CHARACTERS & RELATIONSHIPS

Bram

Key Quotes

'I came to the estate, alone and untroubled by my aloneness, with no greater ambition than to set up a small local paper.' (p.16)

'Yes, I came back, only fools do that, to live among these ruins in a slapped-up shack of leftovers. And for my foolishness I've become the only witness to the final act.' (p.5)

'Don't I say to myself, Bram, take heart, keep faith, this may merely be the prelude of greater things to come?' (p.16)

'[M]e – a fool even unto myself and tired of the farce my life had become.' (p.108)

The reader is not told anything about Bram's life before he moves to the estate, except that he is well educated with an interest in literature. In chapter 2 he characterises himself as a fool for believing the empty promises of the publicity about the housing estate. He describes himself as the 'greatest victim' (p.6) of *ur* because he harbours – until the absolute end of *ur* itself – the belief that it will all work out eventually.

Bram is by nature a solitary character whose life becomes entangled with those around him, forcing him to become part of a wider group when that is not his natural inclination. Referred to by Michael as the "resident intellectual" (p.55), Bram feels a responsibility to produce a newspaper as a way of connecting members of the community. Later, when *ur* has been destroyed, he wishes to record events for posterity.

When he falls in love with Jodie we see his outlook change from being self-contained to constantly desiring her company and dreaming of their future together. For the first time he dreams of a perfect house and family living in suburban bliss, even though he knows this to be an unrealisable fantasy. Love for Jodie skews his attitude towards her father, with unfortunate consequences. He is tolerant of Michael at a time when he should be trying to curtail his excesses for the sake of the other residents. For instance, in conversation with Jodie and Bram, Michael declares that Bram agreed to the wall only because of his love for Jodie:

Through Jodie, Bram finds a degree of comfort and solicitude amid their decaying surroundings. Together they form a unit safe from the world, or so he thinks. His response to her untimely death is characterised by shock and numbness. His description of her appearance on the mortuary slab indicates a certain detachment, an expression of his grief and sense of loss: 'I saw the body, identified her as Jodie and drove back home with the image of her blood-drained face and quiet closed-forever eyes before me' (p.1). He is haunted by her deathly pale face which is marked by scratches, cuts and bruises, testifying to her disastrous journey.

Jodie

Key Quotes

'The daughter left him again and lived (as hearsay had it) a dissolute life of drink, drugs, arguments and abortions ...' (p.28)
'[B]y the simple fact of her arrival a new spirit of enterprise had entered into us.' (p.35)
'She passed by swiftly, cried out softly; I wasn't listening, I couldn't have heard.' (p.145)
'Jodie, growing ever-flatter in my mind, a cigarette paper laid out on a slab, white and so insubstantial that a mere puff of breath might blow her away.' (p.4)

Jodie is characterised as a young woman who has been through some difficult experiences – there are references to her impoverished, sordid life before she moved to *ur* (p.28). She is depicted as a damaged character who is still trying to work out her relationship with her father. Perhaps to make up for their troubles in the past, she is unswervingly loyal to Michael, even when he is obviously leading them into a great deal of trouble. Jodie stays with him, catering to his needs and providing detailed escape plans. However, she soon tires of this life as she becomes ill from her pregnancy, desiring a more stable existence.

When she arrives at the estate, Jodie becomes the 'new force' in everybody's lives. Single-handedly she transforms a bitter winter into a 'kind of spring' (p.35). Jodie prompts a flurry of activity: painting,

planting and repairing. Her presence makes the inhabitants of the estate see themselves differently. While she is not an instigator of these projects, she motivates other people to improve their surroundings.

Jodie is a fairly complex character, but we can only judge her by her actions and appearance. We are never allowed access to the workings of her mind, as we are with the narrator Bram. Jodie is also mysterious to Bram, as she reveals little of her feelings or hopes. An enticing figure, Jodie seems to offer him comfort, yet is unable to love deeply. This inability to be truly intimate with Bram may be because she has been influenced too strongly by her father's destructive passions, to her own detriment.

Her death shows how bound she is to her father and family tradition. The fact that she chooses 'death by misadventure' (as Patterson records it, p.143) over the survival of her newborn child shows that she must have been affected by her family's inherited pessimism. Ironically, she becomes the first female family member actually to carry out her great-grandfather's plans. Her dramatic death symbolises the end of hope and a resignation to the power of tradition over individual agency.

Michael

Key Quotes

'[H]e was perhaps the only original resident of the estate for whom the catalogue of unkept promises meant nothing.' (p.29)

'[H]e flew off again into a series of wild ravings, called for his gun and vowed to go out and attack the invaders that instant in the name of Jodie, his daughter, his son-in-law, Bram, and the grandchildren for which he'd already found names.' (p.104)

One-eyed Michael is a former fencing contractor with a drinking problem who has lost his wife and daughter when he comes to *ur*. He lives on the margins of the community until he helps to build a fence to keep rabbits out of Vito's garden. This is prompted by an important conversation he has with Bram which serves to penetrate (at least to a certain extent) the 'enigma of Michael' (p.28). Before this discussion, he lives on the

margins of the estate, keeping to himself; after it, he is officially inducted into the community (p.30). The arrival of his daughter Jodie also serves to involve him more in the social life of *ur.*

Michael is a very physical character who often intimidates others through his shows of strength. The fact that he is the only resident to carry a rifle means that he exerts a degree of power over the others. The old army jacket and rabbit skin hat that he wears mark him out as a kind of guerrilla fighter, dedicated to the war effort.

Michael's latent madness becomes increasingly apparent during the course of the narrative and it leads others to commit foolhardy acts along with him. The first hint that something is not quite right with Michael occurs to Bram when he notices that Michael is building something out of barbed wire in his shed, but will not acknowledge it to anyone. This turns out to be the barbed wire canoe in which Jodie eventually attempts to float down the creek.

Michael is an anti-social figure who adheres to his own strange code of conduct. Yet he has an overwhelming effect on those around him, contaminating them with his ideas. At one point Bram recognises that Michael's insanity is contagious: 'I could hardly look Craig in the eye, so infected had he become with Michael's madness'(p.108). As well as implicating Craig, Michael also sweeps the other residents up in his wild plans, largely through brute force. Michael also manages to involve his daughter in his dangerous schemes after he leaves *ur,* despite her advancing pregnancy.

As an outlaw, Michael finds support in surprising quarters – two opposing groups, the farmers and the residents' rights activists, support his cause. However, they think of him as a freedom fighter, unaware that he is mad. Michael's outlaw persona is reminiscent of the myth of Ned Kelly, which continued growing in the popular imagination long after his death. Misinterpreted by various parties, Michael's actions grow in importance, despite the fact that they are driven by mania rather than heroism.

Craig

Key Quotes

'One night his random dialling had put him through to a girl – Marie-Claire, he said, and with such lovelorn sincerity that I didn't know whether to laugh or cry – and as stupid as it may have sounded he had fallen head over heels in love with her.' (p.31)

First resident as a squatter, Craig is ushered into the community when he begins to make money for *ur* by selling scrap from the vacant houses. Craig is a vulnerable character who is easily manipulated by others. His character is besmirched by Michael after the vandals' attacks on the estate – Michael assumes that they are old friends of Craig's.

A situation which reveals Craig's innocence occurs when Loch, the government representative, visits the estate. Craig believes every word he says, while the older residents are already inured to the endless fabrications of the authorities. Craig is recruited by Michael and works alongside him until the very end. The two of them try to keep the bulldozers out of the estate by hurling missiles and petrol bombs long after everybody else has ceased trying to resist.

His naivety also has a positive dimension: he is able to love, and receive love from, Marie-Claire. In fact, his relationship with her would never have come about if he was unwilling to take people's words seriously and act on them. By the end of the novel, Craig and Marie-Claire have moved to the French village of Ur – indeed, it may be argued that love saves Craig from harm, while others perish.

Marie-Claire

Key Quotes

'Her parents, he explained, had come from a village of the same name in the Pyrenees, near the border with Spain; she felt as if, by the long way round, she'd returned to her childhood home.' (p.53)

Marie-Claire is a one-dimensional character who doesn't seem to be conflicted in the same way as the major figures in the narrative. A

dedicated nurse and fiancée, she never makes a mistake or acts with questionable motives. She claims that she comes from a small village of the same name in France, so the Australian *ur* is like a second home to her. This aspect of the novel seems entirely implausible, revealing the non-realist elements at work in the text. Along with Vito, Marie-Claire might be read as representing those European migrants in Australia who bring a certain degree of complexity to the culture. Through their efforts these two characters improve conditions for the other residents, but do so without expecting any reward. At the end, Marie-Claire and Craig escape from *ur* before their love is swallowed up by the estate's destruction.

Slug

Key Quotes

'The bar was eventually opened again but not before all trace of Slug's influence had been wiped away: from that day on he became *ur*'s much needed *bête noir*.' (p.52)

'Slug, for motives pure or tainted, was acting as emissary and arbitrator, a last ditch attempt to bring those inside around to reason.' (p.91)

'Slug put his head in his hands and wept; tears streamed down his fat rosy cheeks, his bottom lip blubbered up and down and small drips of saliva fell from it onto the table.' (p.109)

Initially Slug is described as 'undoubtedly the greatest victim' of the collapse of *ur*'s population because his dreams of a local real estate business are destroyed (p.21). However, the collapse of business enables him to enjoy the simpler things in life for a time (p.22). He is a resilient character who follows opportunity at the expense of his relationships. While living in *ur* Slug has a passionate friendship with Dave, with whom he runs the local bar. The intensity of their relationship is registered when Slug departs unexpectedly, leaving Dave in deep mourning. From this day, Slug becomes a traitor in the eyes of the other residents: as Bram remarks, having a shared *bête noir* draws them together.[10]

---

10 'Bête noir' is a French expression meaning a person or thing that one particularly dislikes or dreads.

Slug's later attempt to persuade his former neighbours to give up their battle to stay reinforces their animosity towards him. No-one believes a word he says, but they are held transfixed by 'the gall of the man' (p.91). Michael declares that Slug is "full of lies" like the rest of his government colleagues, and sends him away with a shotgun blast (p.92).

When Bram shows Slug Dave's grave in the Square he is reduced to tears. Bram's unflattering description of this emotional display (p.109) implies that Slug is well fed and soft-hearted, unable to withstand the rigours of resistance. Indeed, he chooses to betray his friends in *ur* rather than stay and fight. In this way, Slug seems to be a fairly amoral character who is primarily concerned with accumulating money and status. By contrast, the remaining residents of *ur* place more emphasis on relationships and a sense of community over financial gain. Slug's value system seems alien and even repugnant to them.

Dave

Key Quotes

''Dave, the last, so overcome with emotion that he could not be moved to speak again.' (p.91)

Dave is known in *ur* for his home-brewed beer, which is a significant consolation during the estate's trials and tribulations. He is depicted as an emotional character who forms a strong bond with Slug, a friendship which allows him to forget about the predicament he is in. This passionate connection is broken when Slug departs suddenly in search of worldly success. Dave takes over the bar from Slug when he leaves, but makes sure that he removes all signs of his former friend. Unlike the others, Dave believed deeply in Slug's trustworthiness and is devastated by his duplicitous actions.

When Slug returns in his new capacity as a government representative and tries to reason with the remaining residents of *ur*, Dave takes it very badly. After this encounter he becomes silent and sits for as many hours as he can at their old table on the footpath outside the bar, like a betrayed lover reliving memories (p.97). It is as if he has pinned all his hopes on

one human being and when this man fails him, he loses faith in human nature as a whole.

Dave's death is essentially caused by his insistence on sitting outside his bar in the open, while aid parcels regularly fall from the sky. He is buried in the middle of the Square because there is nowhere else to put him. The disposal of his body emphasises the uncivilised nature of life in *ur*. The residents have no way of separating the dead from the living, given the fortified state of their territory. Later, the road-builders appear to disturb his grave as they plough their way through the estate, before stopping halfway (p.131).

The representation of Dave's burial evokes the records of the excavation of Ur of the Chaldees, which feature a number of bodies that were placed amongst the living, in the centre of town.

Nanna

Key Quotes

> 'She sat with her back to us, her face to them, in front of the enormous bulldozer at the head of the column. She was still dressed in her blue nylon nightie and held a small posy of flowers in her hand.' (p.94)

The character of Nanna may be derived from the Moon God Nanna (or Nannar) which was worshipped in the original city of Ur. In the novel, Jean, or Nanna as she is known, is a more modest figure. A mother to Alex and flower-seller, she is a sweet-natured resident who represents simple goodness.

Bram describes her flower-selling as 'absurd' and 'monstrous' (p.46) in such a grotesque setting – anywhere else, an old lady selling flowers would be 'the most natural and the most beautiful thing in the world' (p.46). He finds it hard to believe that, despite her desperate circumstances, she continues selling flowers in an attempt to beautify her surroundings. Given her age and frailty, Nanna's heroic stand against the freeway development seems particularly poignant. Of all the crimes perpetrated against the people of *ur*, Nanna's death is perhaps the worst because it is caused by sheer incompetence.

Alex

Key Quotes

"And Alex too ... he's tried his best for his mother's sake but soon he'll be gone and I don't blame him." (Michael, p.101)

Bram (and the reader) comes to know Alex when he is stationed at the tip just outside *ur*'s walls. It turns out that he was once a resident of *ur*, helping his mother at the flower shop. He has been secretly contributing to the estate's activities, repairing Vito's old station wagon in return for bottles of home-brew. As a former insider who then works for the Shire, he has some inkling of what has been planned for *ur*. He acknowledges that the relocation of the tip is part of a larger plan to dislocate the stubborn residents from their homes. In chapter 8, he decides to quit his job and move back inside the estate to help defend it against marauders. Without Alex at the tip, the rubbish piles grow into enormous mountains of waste, showing that he had been working effectively at his job to keep their discomfort to a minimum.

Loyal to the estate while his mother is alive, Alex's sympathies change once she is gone. After Nanna's violent death, Alex exits the estate by driving his bulldozer straight through the South Wall, indicating his distressed state of mind (p.107). Later he takes a job in town and tries to put her death behind him. However, when Bram decides to move back to *ur,* Alex drives him there, showing that he still regards Bram as a friend.

Vito

Key Quotes

'A wiry old Italian with a moustachioed smile whose leftish ideas had apparently got him into some trouble during the war ...'. (p.18)

'He'd apparently left during the night, taking his meagre possessions with him; later that day his tracks were found in the mud by the West Wall and a hand-made ladder was found resting against it.' (p.85)

Vito is a hardworking and resourceful resident of *ur* who departs before the final destruction. In some ways, he is a mysterious figure because we are told little about his past. Bram surmises that his missing finger was lost during the war, but does not know any more details. From the brief description we are given, we assume that he is an Italian migrant who has saved carefully to buy his house at the estate, only to find that it is a planning disaster. However, he makes the best of the situation, keeping the other residents fed through hard winters with his gardening.

In keeping with his communist leanings, Vito is the one who proposes the idea of pooling resources in order to live more comfortably. Unlike Michael, who infects people with his negative attitudes, Vito's 'spirit of enterprise' is infectious in a positive sense, spurring his neighbours to contribute to the common good (p.19). As a survivor of the war, he has a realistic view of the ongoing conflict between *ur* and the bulldozers. Thus, when he realises the fight is almost over, he leaves quietly in the night before matters get worse.

THEMES & ISSUES

The power of rumour

Key Quotes

"It's a remarkable wall, don't get me wrong, more amazing by far than even rumour had suggested ..." (Loch, p.76)

'Rumours of his exploits spread, and though people began speculating wildly on the reasons for them, no-one but the cognizant few ever managed to connect the story back to the destruction of *ur*.' (p.120)

The residents of *ur* live in a perpetual state of expectation, based on the whisperings that emanate from outside and the dreams originating from inside their walls. Cut off from modern communications networks, they rely on old-fashioned word-of-mouth, which tends to distort the facts in the act of communication. Neglected by the authorities and isolated from the rest of society, the people of *ur* are apt to invent theories to explain their dire situation.

Michael and Jodie's criminal exploits are supported by farmers and, later, suburban activists, based on rumours that he is crusading for their causes, when in fact he is on his own personal journey, motivated more by his deepening madness than his sense of duty to others. Like Ned Kelly, Michael is transformed into a mythical figure by the rumours which have spread about his outrageous deeds. The persistence of these rumours suggests that when people want to believe in a hero they will often choose not to take in any evidence to the contrary.

When he is living at the pub, Bram is supported by the kindness of well-wishers who believe that he is a friend of Michael's. After accepting their generosity for a time, Bram finally reveals the truth to Patterson, the police sergeant: "The sooner he's caught the better as far as I'm concerned. And tell all these people here that I'm neither his friend nor theirs" (p.127). This statement has the desired effect, disproving the rumours which had circulated around him and ridding him of friendships offered under false pretences. Recognising that his position at the pub is now precarious, Bram decides to return to the site of his recent trauma.

It is here that he attempts to recuperate the story of *ur*, which is already beginning to fade from people's minds.

Much of Bram's narrative is composed of rumours because nobody else is available to provide a first-hand account. The others have either departed or died, so Bram is obliged to write their stories on their behalf. He creates a dramatic tale from the narrative pieces he has gleaned through conversations and hearsay.

The importance of dreams

Key Quotes

'If we could have held that moment, frozen it in time, shut out all the sights and sounds that suggested disintegration and ruin, we might yet have believed in our dreams and seen long, contented lives ahead of us.' (p.97)

"Forget everything else, it must be simplified to this: two couples, two homes, in which two families can be raised." (Michael, p.102)

"You've got to know when to give up hoping, that's the art of happy living, as far as I'm concerned." (Tony, p.116)

Most of the long-term residents of *ur* are driven there by various past problems. As Michael puts it: "I began my time here with so many hopes, like so many of us, running from an unhappy past to a new and unknown future" (p.100). Like Michael, the other residents buy houses in the estate to escape from unhappiness, in search of fulfilment and a better quality of life. When these dreams do not eventuate, many residents continue to pin their hopes on the prospect of rescue, either by the government or through their own actions.

Each person has their own particular set of desires. Bram, for instance, wants to settle down with Jodie, all the while knowing that this is unlikely to happen. Nanna dreams of running a successful flower shop that provides her neighbours with fresh blooms throughout the year. Dave wants to run a successful bar with his friend, Slug. Vito attempts to feed the entire estate with his fruitful garden. Even 'mad' Michael dreams of creating a safe environment in which the two young couples can raise children.

In conversation with Bram at the pub, Tony, the cleaner, declares that hope sustains people. Despite the setbacks he has experienced, Tony finds it impossible to give up his dream of obtaining more building work. He suspects that he will be working at the pub for the rest of his life, but he also knows the value of harbouring a dream. Bram describes him as a 'bricklayer-in-waiting' who is probably 'the most deluded of us all' (p.118). Yet the old bricklayer helps Bram to realise his plan of returning to live in *ur* by building a shack out of leftover materials. Later, Tony provides Bram with a reason to leave and to seek a new future at Haranhope by working as Tony's assistant.

Key Point

Despite his innate optimism, Bram considers that Tony is 'deluded' because of his unrealistic hopes for the future. Through Tony's character, the text suggests that a certain level of delusion may be necessary in order to survive hardships and preserve one's sense of identity.

Bureaucratic corruption

Key Quotes

'We still had no idea what the visit was about but we had become so used to bad news that I suppose we were all taking this moment to prepare ourselves for the worst.' (p.73)

"There was never any plan for a satellite town, much less a plan to build a one hundred kilometre stretch of freeway, the cost of which, by my calculations, would consume two and a half times the Department's current budget." (Loch, p.77)

Bram conveys his suspicion of bureaucracy after the opening of the estate. The Premier describes the estate as 'a model of things to come' (p.8) in his opening speech. However, Bram suspects that the residents are in fact 'guinea pigs' (p.7) in a social experiment. The estate is government-subsidised, allowing even those who are less well-off to afford their own suburban house, but it also relies on other resources for its future success. From the beginning, *ur*'s future is dependent on the construction of a freeway linking it to the city. The promise of the freeway is one of the

most important factors governing the residents' decisions to move there, along with petrol discounts. When the freeway does not eventuate, the residents begin to understand that the government does not always fulfil its promises. The burning of an effigy of a bureaucrat, complete with suit, tie and cardboard briefcase, shows the residents' deep distrust of authority figures (p.23).

The inhabitants of *ur* are lied to so often that they lose all belief in what outsiders tell them. Failing to acknowledge its former mistakes and make amends, the government blames the inhabitants of *ur* for their own plight. It sends a series of spokesmen to persuade the people of *ur* to leave. Layland is the first government representative who attempts to negotiate with the residents. He is held captive after being injured by Michael, providing the residents with a useful bargaining item. Unfortunately, this does not have the desired effect because it appears that nobody misses him: 'Far from being the insurance policy we had thought him to be, it seemed in fact that to his employers Layland was completely expendable' (p.68).

By the time Loch arrives with his two security guards, the only person who believes him is the 'innocent' Craig, who hangs on Loch's every word (p.85). The author represents the speeches from the government officials Layland, Loch and Slug in detail, showing how their language works to deceive people. Loch's speech is remarkable for the way he manages to shift blame onto other entities, rather than shouldering the responsibility for the failure of *ur* and its residents' suffering himself. He itemises all their grievances to give the impression that he is on their side, but reneges on his promises. He flinches, momentarily (p.82) when Michael makes him sign a written account of his speech, as he knows that what he has said is untrue.

As well as being a fable of human drama on the scale of individuals, *Blueprints for a Barbed-Wire Canoe* also tells a larger story about institutional forces lining up against ordinary people, forcing them to comply with the wishes and agendas of bodies such as governments and councils. The state has many more resources at its disposal than the embattled residents who are scraping a living from the land. This is an

uneven match from the start, but the remaining residents put up a valiant fight, against the odds.

Optimism versus pessimism

Key Quotes

'The original dream was shattered, all but the deluded had fled ....' (p.14)
'All abandoned; all pointless, useless, an ugly scar to an ugly wound.' (p.132)
'All in all, by the time the true spring arrived, we were riding a cresting wave of optimism; the future was before us, a mismanaged past behind.' (p.35)
'She remembered well enough my talk of high ideals, grand hopes and new beginnings; her look impaled me for an instant to those hollow words then burst them like an arrow to a hot air balloon.' (p.74)

Bram, the narrator, is an optimist who is gradually worn down during the course of the story. The bureaucrats who try to reason with the residents are deliberately misleading, turning the inhabitants of *ur* into jaded observers. Nonetheless, and despite their considerable hardships, Bram and the other residents are able to find beauty in their surroundings. For instance, they appreciate the simple beauty of the night sky as they sit drinking in the Square: 'The evenings fell slowly ... clear as we were of the city lights, night revealed above us a magic cupola of stars' (p.15). Denied basic human services, the residents of *ur* seek solace in each other's company and the contemplation of natural events.

Housing developments are often advertised as little utopias which you can join if you have sufficient money. The decaying estate of Macauley's novel might be seen as a reaction against this kind of false utopianism, suggesting instead that optimism struggles to survive in such straitened circumstances. Bodies and spirits are crushed in the battle to save decrepit dwellings from demolition. The home-owners hang grimly onto their 'dreams' until the bitter end, as if their home-ownership was an indispensable aspect of their identities.

The blueprints that Michael gives to Bram express a sense of life's futility. They instruct the canoeist to recite the prayer 'Nothing matters, i don't care' three times every hour, claiming that more this will provide them with strength (p.105). The main requirement of this seemingly pointless

exercise is that it be done in a dignified manner 'with head held high' (p.105). The blueprints present this nihilistic act as an antidote for a person who is 'sick of life' (p.104): leaving the world in such a manner is supposed to provide the canoeist with a sense of purpose denied to them by life's vicissitudes. Yet it is clearly a destructive act which hurts those left behind, perpetuating a bizarre family tradition.

Key Point

Through his description of the contents of the blueprints, *Macauley* suggests that despairing optimists may become pessimists driven to desperate acts once all hope is gone. In another possible interpretation, the blueprints could be read as suggesting that an optimistic outlook which is blind to reality is ultimately self-destructive.

The value of community

Key Quotes

'We'd left them all behind; uncles, aunts, cousins too; we had each other, and it was a family of sorts, but the sight of Michael and Jodie often cruelly reminded us that any family, no matter how bonded, interdependent and happy is an ersatz family compared to the one linked by blood.' (p.35)

As conditions in *ur* worsen, the inhabitants become emotionally bonded to one another. The exception to this pattern is Michael, who remains on the outside of these inter-relationships to a certain extent. Yet it is his troubled relationship with his daughter Jodie which makes the others miss the families they have left behind. When she appears, Jodie seems to complete Michael's life. He explains that her return has reinforced his wavering commitment to *ur*: "I had my daughter, I *had* family, and this was enough to convince me to stay" (p.100). Jodie and Michael's reunion reminds the others of the families they have lost, spurring them to act together as a unit. Thrown together by circumstance, this odd collection of people becomes more coherent as they become intimate with each other.

The residents of *ur* share their resources and make decisions together after Vito, the old communist, breaks the ice' (p.18). Vito suggests that the estate residents pool their wealth in an effort to endure their impoverished isolation. He begins by setting an example: he grows vegetables and sells them in town for the benefit of the community. Bram distributes a leaflet explaining the new financial arrangements proposed by Vito, then the others follow suit, contributing what they can to the group funds.

The community is also brought together through their drinking sessions at the bar. Dave's home-brew allows them to unwind and forget the misery of their living conditions: All was drunkenness, foolishness, frivolity; clinking bottles, breaking glasses, laughing, shouting; a cacophony of noise under a still, solid sky' (p.23). Away from established society, they construct their own rules of conduct, some of which may seem strange to outsiders.

Bram's newspaper also serves to connect people in the community. What he writes is not journalism but another kind of writing suited to the needs and hopes of his neighbours. Readers anxiously wait for each issue to arrive and praise its contents when it does (p.26). Through these common rituals the inhabitants of *ur* experience a sense of harmony for a time, until they are divided by Michael's bullying behaviour.

Macauley's characters are very resilient in their opposition to the forces that threaten to extinguish their community. Given the pressures exerted against them, their survival for several years is impressive. It is their ability to cooperate with and support each other that enables them to rise above every blow.

Key Point

The novel shows that even when people's material possessions are stripped from them, they can retain a fighting spirit that defies the odds – a spirit that is enhanced by a sense of community.

Overdevelopment of the landscape

Key Quotes

"We'll be spreading out, expanding, until the end of time. And we won't rest happy till we've filled all that up too." (Michael, p.83)

The novel suggests that the human desire to extend the cityscape into any vacant land is due to a fear of the nothingness beyond the boundaries of the known. It implies that unused land is seen as a threat by Australians, who regard it as blank space that needs to be filled with new developments.

Even mad Michael can see the folly of the endless expansion of housing onto farmland. In a moment of clarity he expounds on how people in estates like *ur* are ghettoised and forgotten by society's

regulating, institutional powers (p.83). He criticises the desire to use all available space rather than to appreciate the land as it is:

> "the fact is you either get on with your neighbours or you don't. And if you don't, and that's usually the case, you'll do whatever you can to get as far away from them as possible. There'll be estates, suburbs, towns like this sprouting up like mushrooms across the universe for the next ten billion years." (p.83)

Here Michael characterises estates as being part of the human drive to avoid dealing with difficult social relations. Attracted to the new development at first, the residents become victims of its faulty design. The freeway development, once so desired, instead becomes a direct threat to the community. When it eventually comes it is aimed at the estate, threatening to demolish the residents' homes. There is a great irony in the fact that the very thing they want actually destroys them. Bram points out the injustice of another estate being given the freeway that was designated for *ur*. What most disturbs him is that the new residents take it for granted, as a right, while the residents of *ur* have had to survive without it.

Key Point

Macauley cautions against filling up all available land with housing because it can lead to the ghettoisation of suburban populations.

Writing as a reflection on experience

Key Quotes

'The estate, its inhabitants, and the terrible tale of its destruction may end up as little more than a footnote in history but if I didn't write that footnote, who would?' (p.138)

'[W]hatever little gaps remained in the tale I could fill with fantasy and fiction.'(p.141)

Bram's tale attempts to redeem the horrific history of *ur*, turning a pitiable story into a heroic one. His relentless sifting through the remains of the estate alludes to the excavations of the original 'Ur of the Chaldees', which has been studied by various archaeologists in an attempt to reveal its secrets. Like its ancient equivalent, *ur* comprises layers from different

periods of habitation. These layers contain a number of objects that symbolise aspects of the collective life of *ur*, which Bram is attempting to reconstruct.

Bram believes that the heroic struggle of the residents of *ur* will be obscured if he does not record it for posterity. It pains him to think that the efforts of his neighbours will amount to nothing if he does not immortalise them in print. At the same time, he recognises the inevitable distortions involved in trying to represent the thoughts, experiences and hopes of others. He wrestles with the severe writer's block that is caused by his anxiety about misrepresenting the estate and its former inhabitants. He doubts the value of his own reflections, censoring his recollections as he writes. In the end he decides to continue with the writing process, despite his misgivings: 'To hell with it anyway! I heard my mind saying; who but you will ever know if the story rings true or not?' (p.144). In other words, there are no remaining witnesses to critique his version of events, so he may as well write it from his own perspective.

Through the writing process, Bram reflects on the past and his attempts to record it, criticising himself for inaction. He asks himself why he didn't hear Jodie cry out as she passed his shack on the way to her death. He concludes that he didn't hear her because he was 'watching the fragments of my story fly up from my table like so many startled starlings from a tree' (p.145). That is, instead of trying to save her, he is busily immortalising her on the page at the time of her death.

Bram's struggle to write the story of *ur* may mirror the author's own experience of producing this novel. A painstaking process which took ten years to complete, the writing of *Blueprints for a Barbed-Wire Canoe* parallels the composition of Bram's narrative about *ur*. It is a story in a story that allows Macauley to offer a commentary on the difficulty of recording experience truthfully and the anxieties which accompany this endeavour. While Macauley's novel is pure fiction, the writing of it may have been as taxing as Bram's first-person narrative is depicted as being.

Key Point

Bram's narrative stands witness to the vexed history of ur, *making it an important historical document, a salutary fable about the perils of overdevelopment, Bram's text warns its readers not to repeat the same mistakes*

Decay

Key Quotes

'Though the sewage produced by a mere seven individuals may be rightly considered a trifle, it was more than enough to infect the slow-moving creek and the market garden with a rich rotting smell that often and particularly in summer hung over the northern part of *ur* like a poisonous cloud.' (p.25–6)

'Our little village, our little piece of suburban paradise, had become an inglorious shambles.' (p.72)

'Layland's gangrenous leg was gone, Marie-Claire had performed the operation with a carving knife and hacksaw and Layland had suffered it uncomplainingly, knowing death to be the only alternative.' (p.73)

'The wall might be a protection against the vandals and any other form of violent assault but it could nothing to stop the slow rot that was now eating us away from the inside.' (p.67)

Images of decay recur throughout Macauley's text, serving to draw the reader's attention to the dystopian nature of *ur*. According to his author statements, Macauley aims to critique the taken-for-granted positive evaluation of suburbia of many Australians.[11] By charting the destruction of a purpose-built community, he shows how nature can so easily take over any built environment. The land and the elements assert themselves at the expense of the flimsy dwellings, which quickly collapse. The level of decay is exaggerated for dramatic effect, accelerating a process which might take much longer in reality.

Almost from the beginning the residents of *ur* are surrounded by sewage. Later, a rubbish dump is created in close proximity to the estate, bombarding the residents with foul smells: 'the pile soon grew into an enormous rotting mountain of waste whose unbearable stench was wafted across *ur* on the breeze'(p.68). Bram has a moment of epiphany about *ur* as he is talking to Alex, the tip assistant. He suddenly sees how degraded the estate has become and acknowledges the depths to which they have sunk, through official neglect. He feels overwhelmed by this knowledge and experiences it as a bout of nausea:

---

11 See Macauley, 'Where do I come from?', http://members.dodo.com.au/~ghannah/macauley.html.

> There was the foul taste of a hangover in my mouth and my clothes gave off a faint whiff of kerosene. The smell of the newly dumped load of rubbish made me turn away to retch. (p.47)

Most of the time, the inhabitants of *ur* are used to the stench but it strikes visitors more powerfully. When they are visited by Loch and the guards, the narrator describes their appearance as being like 'the sweet perfume of a bunch of flowers' after being shut up in a 'musty room' (p.72). Although the reality of their condition is infinitely worse, he chooses to describe their situation using metaphors.

The estate, which was created as an experiment in modern living, becomes a "blot on the landscape" (p.46) after a short time, due to its structural shortcomings. From its inception as a celebrated new housing complex, it is soon transformed into an eyesore, overgrown and stinking. The residents' dreams of a comfortable future are rapidly dashed, replaced by a life of bare subsistence amid squalor. The pressure they are put under reduces their morale to such an extent that they turn against each other and give up their dreams. The text argues that isolated communities can become stronger, developing a sense of solidarity, but they can also decay through neglect.

The unseen 'vandals' who terrorise the community contribute to the idea that *ur*'s demise cannot be halted. At first the residents ignore these small acts of destruction, but then the vandals' nightly invasions suddenly turn nasty. Their attacks become so systematic that Bram and the others begin to think that the vandals are working for the authorities that wish to be rid of an embarrassing eyesore. As the vandals destroy anything they can, the residents begin to feel increasingly embattled. The fact that outside forces are working to ruin their estate makes them feel less inclined to do anything productive, contributing to a sense of inevitably increasing entropy.

Absent children

Key Quotes

"Look at it: a barren, childless place … There can never be children here, and without children, a new generation in which to pour all our hopes and dreams, the rot in *ur's* heart will eat it away." (Bram to Alex, p.46)

'I'd woken with her image before me again, the cold white face, the matted hair, her stomach so flat that it almost looked shrunken; the great fertile hump she'd been carrying, gone.'(p.4)

Families with children depart first, leaving an atomised bunch of individuals who have their own reasons for remaining in *ur*. Bram sees the lack of children as a sign of decay, because children symbolise a link with the future and are vessels for the hopes and dreams of adults. Ghostly children appear throughout the novel, in the imaginings of Bram and Michael. Michael hopes for a future in *ur* sustained by the two young couples and their children, even though it is no place for raising families. Similarly, Bram imagines a rosy suburban future with Jodie and their child, despite her obvious unwillingness to 'settle down'. After her death, he thinks of their dead child, left lying in a paddock, surrounded by cows. This 'blue grey bundle of flesh' (p.143), his dead child, signals the end of these impossible fantasies.

Essentially, their baby is a victim of Michael's inherited blueprints, because Jodie sought to follow this grisly tradition instead of raising her own child. As a young woman she lives a rough life, punctuated by abortions and drug-taking. This sets the scene for her later actions, suggesting that she does not have well-developed maternal instincts. This unfulfilled promise of new life leaves the narrator feeling bereft and devoid of hope. Somewhere on the other side of the world, the other young couple, Craig and Marie-Claire, may raise a child, far from the depredations of the Australian *ur*. Theirs is the only success story to be found in the novel, since those who stay are forced to pay a substantial price for the failure of the estate.

Key Point

The absence of children from the estate indicates that the community will be short-lived because it cannot regenerate itself.

QUESTIONS & ANSWERS

The text response questions on the examination paper are divided into two groups. Each group requires a different approach. The first group requires an interpretative response to the text and focuses on characters, relationships, style, structure and narrative. The second group calls for a discussion of the themes and issues, values, social perspectives and the unstated views that texts may embody through their representations of people, events, issues and ideas. This group relates to the wider implications of the text.

Part 1 exam topics

1 Bram describes himself as "a fool even unto myself and tired of the farce my life had become".
Is this your view of Bram?

2 "If we could have held that moment, frozen it in time ... we might yet have believed in our dreams and seen long, contented lives ahead of us."
How does Bram's love for Jodie change his perceptions of the world around him?

3 'Jodie consistently rejects the conventional roles that are assigned to her.'
Discuss.

4 'Bram and Jodie's relationship promises more than it delivers.'
Discuss.

5 'Michael is a very physical character, who intimidates rather than inspires others.'
Do you agree?

6 'The original dream was shattered, all but the deluded had fled ...'
Are the remaining inhabitants of *ur* deluded or merely optimistic?

Part 2 exam topics

1 '*Blueprints for a Barbed-Wire Canoe* shows that when people endure hardships, a sense of community provides a source of consolation.' Discuss.

2 '*Blueprints for a Barbed-Wire Canoe* shows that overdevelopment of the landscape may be detrimental to Australian society.' Do you agree?

3 "The estate, its inhabitants, and the terrible tale of its destruction may end up as little more than a footnote in history but if I didn't write that footnote, who would?"
'The text suggests that the recording of human experience is a complex blend of fiction and fact.'
Discuss.

4 '*Blueprints for a Barbed-Wire Canoe* challenges the suburban dream by representing the dramatic disintegration of a new housing estate.' Discuss.

5 'The text shows that even when people's material possessions are stripped from them, they can retain a fighting spirit that defies the odds.'
Discuss.

Sample analysis of a part 2 topic

1 '*Blueprints for a Barbed-Wire Canoe* shows that when people endure hardships, a sense of community provides a source of consolation.' Discuss.

In the introduction discuss the key terms 'hardships', 'community' and 'consolation'. Briefly indicate which hardships and instances of community you will discuss in the body of the essay. The extent to which the inhabitants of *ur* are actually comforted by a sense of togetherness needs to be considered. Does this apply to all the residents or only some of them? What is meant by the term, 'consolation'?

Frame your response in terms of agreement or disagreement with the main contention of the question. Say why you agree/disagree with it (this is your argument).

Approach 1: agreement with the contention

- In the body of the essay, explain what hardships the residents have to endure, such as being isolated from the rest of society, surrounded by rubbish and sewage, having no water or electricity, being attacked by vandals and neglected by the authorities. How do these experiences impact on the ways in which the characters relate to one another? The residents of the estate are thrown together through their shared experience of oppression – is this enough to bind them together forever?
- Consider the question of 'community'. How is this manifested in the characters' interactions? What aspects of life in *ur* function to connect people? You might explore the elements that bring them together, such as the local newspaper written by Bram, Slug and Dave's bar and Vito's vegetable patch, which requires a considerable effort to maintain. Through their shared experiences of these things, the people of *ur* begin to appreciate the beauty of their environment, rather than focusing on the negative aspects.
- Next you should explain how community activities can make the residents feel better about their predicament. Can you think of any particular instances that exemplify their concern for each other? How do these moments make their lives more bearable? Here you might suggest Vito's vegetable gardening as an example of a generous gesture which ensures the residents receive fresh food. Or you could cite Craig's trips to town to phone his French girlfriend as an instance where an individual's needs are met through group consensus.
- Recognition of possible counter examples to your argument will contribute to a more nuanced essay. For instance, you might acknowledge that not all the residents are working for the common cause. Slug betrays the other residents by working for the government, while Michael causes considerable destruction through

his efforts to defend the estate. These figures indicate that there are significant divisions in the community of *ur*.

- To resolve this discussion you could suggest that, while a sense of community can make the residents feel less unhappy (thereby acting as a source of consolation), it cannot completely compensate them for their material deprivations. Their pooling of resources and energies may help them survive for a few years but ultimately it cannot save them from the forces which seek to destroy the estate.

Approach 2: disagreement with the contention

You could make the following points to indicate that a sense of community cannot compensate for the wrongs done to the inhabitants of *ur*.

- Firstly, *ur* does not have a continuously coherent communal atmosphere. During the course of the novel, the community undergoes a number of significant transformations. There are alliances between characters like Bram and Jodie which work against the common good. For instance, Bram's love for Jodie blinds him to the potentially destructive effects of the building of Michael's wall.
- The residents of the estate do not always act in the best interests of the group. As conditions worsen, characters like Vito and Alex opt out altogether, leaving *ur* in order to save themselves. Slug departs early in the narrative to further his career, at the expense of his friendship with Dave. On a number of occasions, personal choices are made which clash with the needs of the community as a whole.
- Two characters, Dave and Nanna, are killed through preventable accidents. If the others had been more vigilant and concerned with their neighbours' wellbeing these accidents may not have happened.
- Michael thinks he is working to save the estate from destruction, but he is responsible for much of the damage which is done to the other residents. He is the most unpredictable element of *ur*'s community, disregarding the wishes of others in his drive to build a suburban idyll. Michael is immune to the desires of his fellow residents due to his increasing madness.

- To conclude, bring together the evidence provided in the body of the essay to reinforce the idea that the people of *ur* have a fragmented community which offers inconsistent levels of support. For this reason, their sense of community cannot be considered a real consolation for their squalid living conditions. Explain how both internal conflict and outside pressures work to undermine any communal enterprise in the estate. Restate the argument and finish with a clear and incisive response to the question.

REFERENCES & READING

Text

Macauley, Wayne. *Blueprints for a Barbed-Wire Canoe*, Black Pepper, Melbourne, 2004.

Website

Kyriacou, Kate 'Writer tells of urban myth', Moreland Leader, 15 March 2004. Available online at http://members.dodo.com.au/~ghannah/macauleybfabwc.html#Interview

Macauley, '*Where do I come from*?' Available online at http://members.dodo.com.au/~ghannah/macauley.html

Rivers, Bronwyn '*A descent into the wildness of isolation*', Sydney Morning Herald, 5–6 June 2004. Available online at http://members.dodo.com.au/~ghannah/macauleybfabwc.html

Rundle, Guy launch speech (n.d.). Available online at http://members.dodo.com.au/~ghannah/macauleybfabwc.html

The Black Pepper website (http://members.dodo.com.au/~ghannah/macauleybfabwc.html) offers a number of other useful reviews of *Blueprints for a Barbed-Wire Canoe* as well as author interviews.

Other Titles in this Series

A Lesson Before Dying
A View from the Bridge
Angela's Ashes
The Baghdad Blog
Blade Runner
Blueprints for a Barbed-Wire Canoe
Border Crossing
Breaker Morant
Brilliant Lies
Cabaret
Dead Letter Office
Diving for Pearls
Don't Start Me Talking Lyrics 1984–2004
Dream Stuff
Falling
Fine Line
First They Killed My Father
Fly Away Peter
Gattaca
Generals Die in Bed
Girl with a Pearl Earring
Going Home
Hamlet
Henry Lawson's Short Stories
I for Isobel
If This is a Man
I'm Not Scared
Inheritance
In the Lake of the Woods
Jackson's Track
Lantana
Life of Galileo
Maestro
Macbeth
Medea
Minimum of Two
Montana 1948
Night
No Great Mischief
Oedipus the King
One True Thing
Only the Heart
Othello
Romulus, My Father
Selected Poems (Sylvia Plath)
Shakespeare in Love
Stolen
Sky Burial
Tess of the D'Urbervilles
The Accidental Tourist
The Age of Innocence
The Chant of Jimmie Blacksmith
The Curious Incident of the Dog in the Night-time
The Divine Wind
The Freedom of the City
The Great Gatsby
The Hunter
The Kite Runner
The Longest Memory
The Outsider
The Penguin Book of First World War Poetry
The Plague
The Player
The Quiet American
The Stories of Tobias Wolff
The Things They Carried
The Third Man
The Wife of Martin Guerre
The Year of Living Dangerously
Things Fall Apart
Triage
What's Eating Gilbert Grape?